Moose the Mouse

Likes to Run

Moose the Mouse
Likes to Run

Written by G. E. Miller

Illustrated by Paul James Valencia

Butterfly Typeface Publishing
PO Box 56193
Little Rock, AR 72215

This book is dedicated to two people who I love so much, my mother and my husband.

To my mother, the greatest storyteller I know. She could write a 'best seller' if she just took the time to write it.

And to my husband, my greatest supporter! Always applauding and encouraging me to step out of my shell and into my gift.

This is a story about
a Mouse named Moose
who likes to run ...

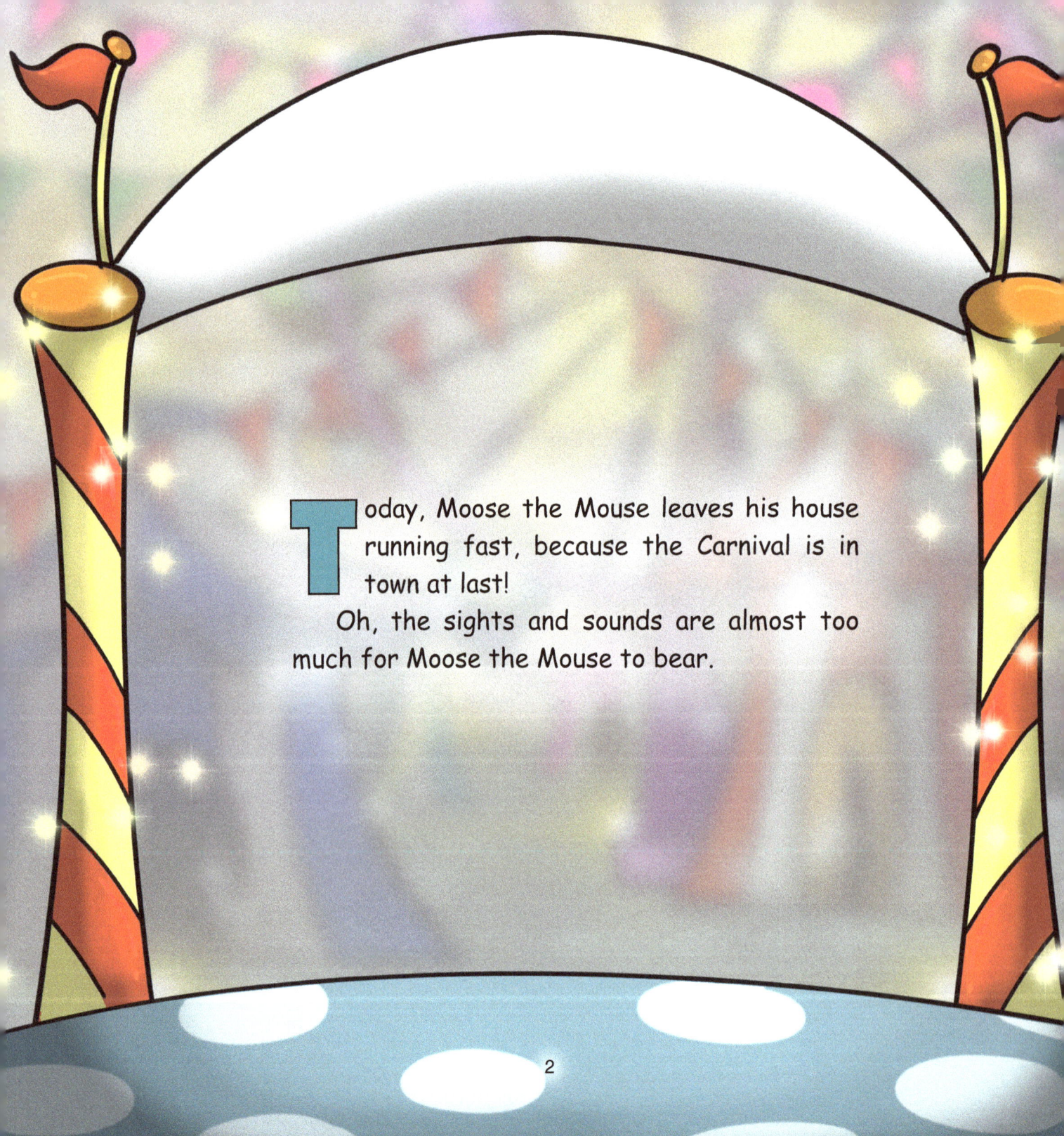

Today, Moose the Mouse leaves his house running fast, because the Carnival is in town at last!

Oh, the sights and sounds are almost too much for Moose the Mouse to bear.

CARNIVAL

And the best part is that his friend Kitty the Kitten is waiting for him there!

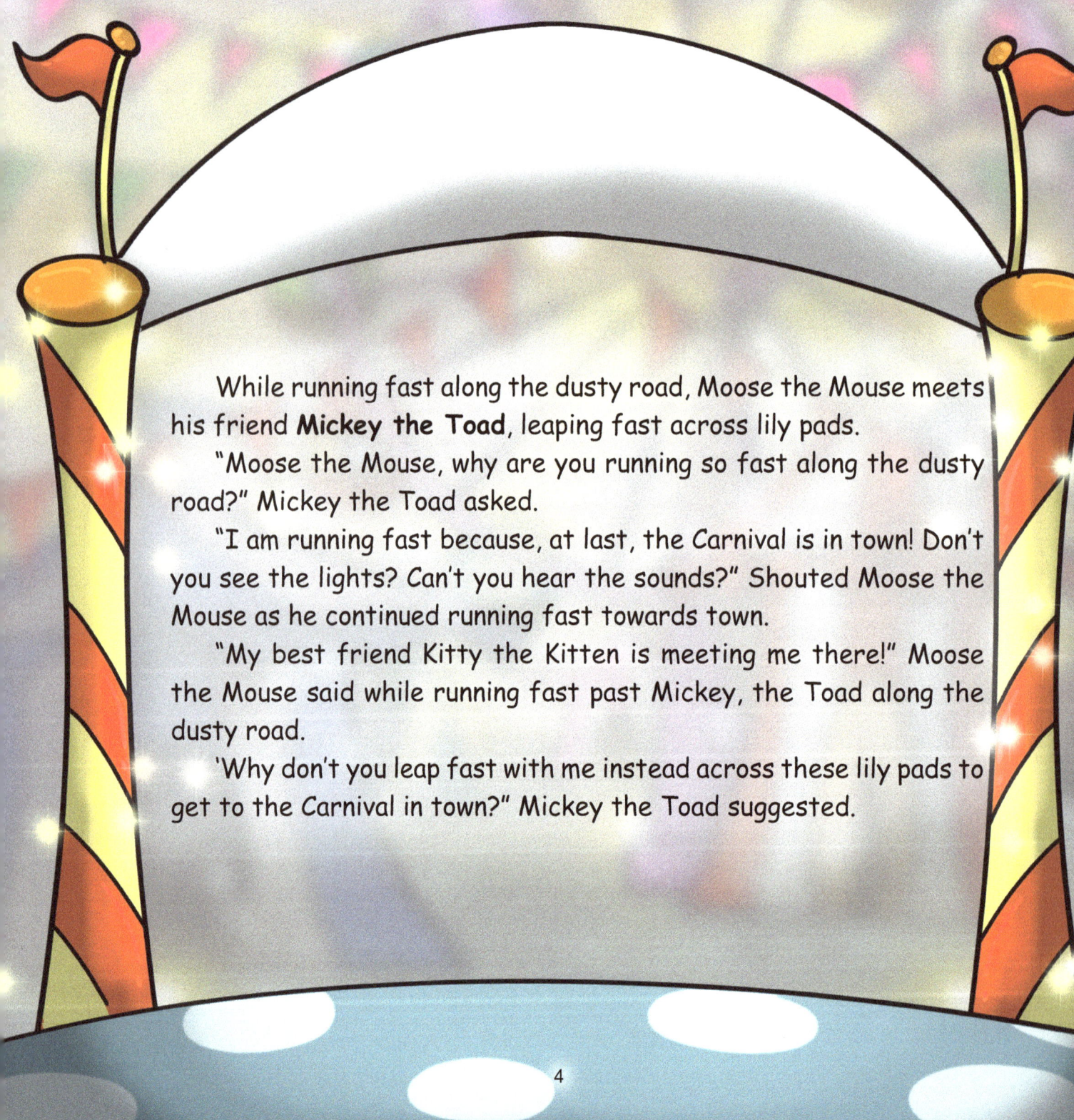

While running fast along the dusty road, Moose the Mouse meets his friend **Mickey the Toad**, leaping fast across lily pads.

"Moose the Mouse, why are you running so fast along the dusty road?" Mickey the Toad asked.

"I am running fast because, at last, the Carnival is in town! Don't you see the lights? Can't you hear the sounds?" Shouted Moose the Mouse as he continued running fast towards town.

"My best friend Kitty the Kitten is meeting me there!" Moose the Mouse said while running fast past Mickey, the Toad along the dusty road.

'Why don't you leap fast with me instead across these lily pads to get to the Carnival in town?" Mickey the Toad suggested.

"Even though I like to run, leaping fast can be lots of fun! So I will leap with you across lily pads to get to the Carnival in town." Moose the Mouse said.

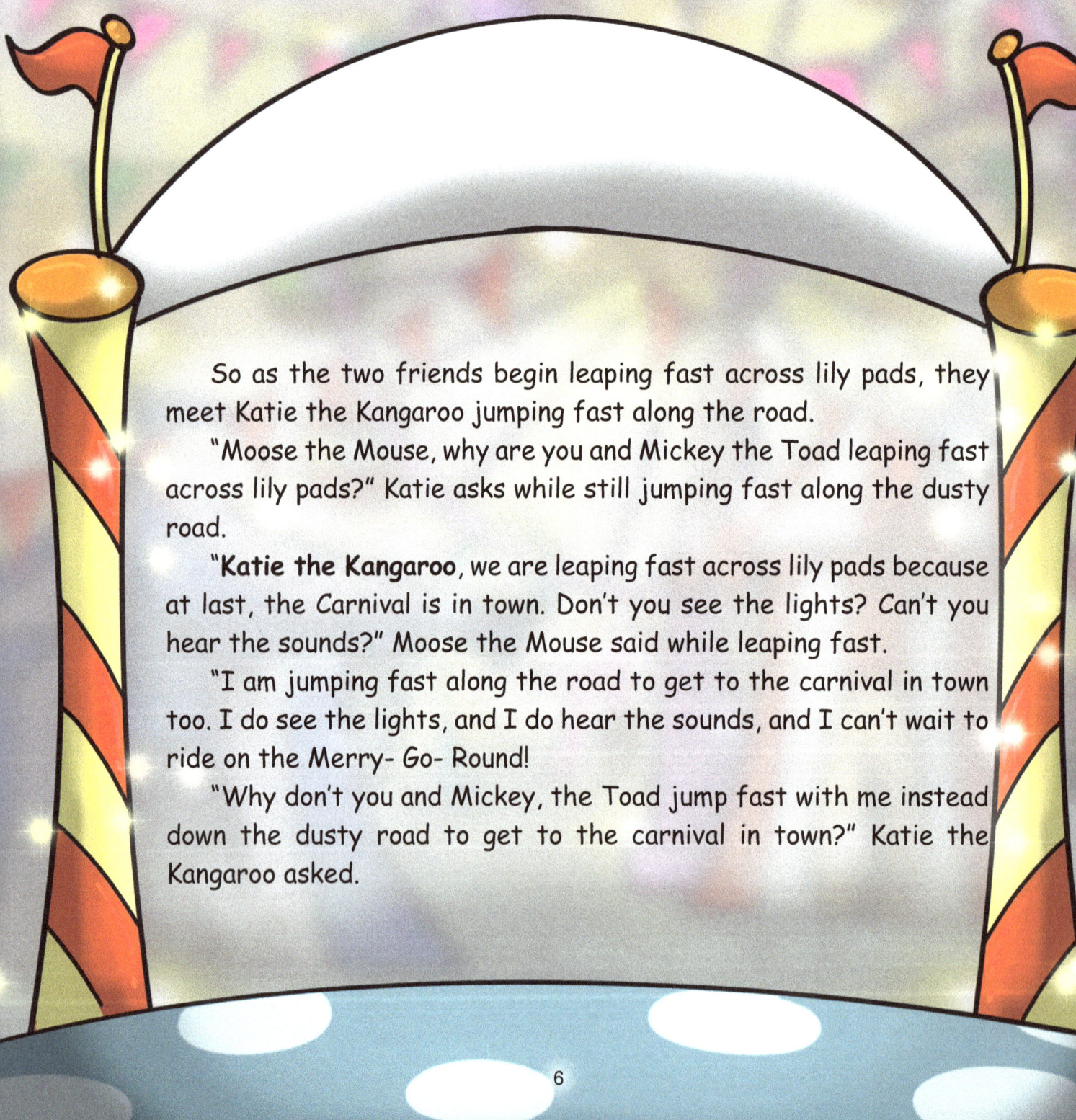

So as the two friends begin leaping fast across lily pads, they meet Katie the Kangaroo jumping fast along the road.

"Moose the Mouse, why are you and Mickey the Toad leaping fast across lily pads?" Katie asks while still jumping fast along the dusty road.

"**Katie the Kangaroo**, we are leaping fast across lily pads because at last, the Carnival is in town. Don't you see the lights? Can't you hear the sounds?" Moose the Mouse said while leaping fast.

"I am jumping fast along the road to get to the carnival in town too. I do see the lights, and I do hear the sounds, and I can't wait to ride on the Merry- Go- Round!

"Why don't you and Mickey, the Toad jump fast with me instead down the dusty road to get to the carnival in town?" Katie the Kangaroo asked.

"Even though I really like to run, I know that jumping fast along the dusty road can be lots of Fun! So we will jump fast with you along the dusty road to get to the carnival in town," Moose the Mouse agreed.

So, the three friends, Moose the Mouse, Mickey the Toad, and Katie the Kangaroo began jumping fast down the road to get to the carnival in town.

While jumping fast, they passed **Bunny the Rabbit** packing a head of fresh green cabbage from her grandmother's vegetable patch into a brown paper lunch sack.

"Why are the three of you jumping fast like kangaroos down the road?" Bunny the Rabbit asked.

"We are jumping fast because, at last, the Carnival is in town! Can't you see the lights and hear the sounds?" Moose the Mouse replied while jumping fast.

"Kitty, the Kitten, is waiting for him there," the two friends shouted!

"Yes, I see the lights, and I hear the sounds, and I can't wait to see all the funny clowns," Bunny the Rabbit replied.

"Why don't you guys hop fast with me along the grass to get to the carnival in town?" She suggested.

"Even though I like to run, I know that hopping fast along the grass can be lots of Fun! So we will hop with you along the grass to get to the carnival in town." Moose the Mouse agreed.

So, now all four friends, Moose the Mouse, Mickey the Toad, Katie the Kangaroo, and Bunny the Rabbit, were hopping fast across the grass to get to the carnival in town when they met **Stanley the Turtle** slowly strolling around with a somewhat sad frown.

He did not hesitate to ask, "Why are you all hopping fast along the grass?"

"We are hopping fast because, at last, the carnival is in town!" The four friends shouted.

"Kitty the Kitten is waiting for Moose the Mouse there," Mickey the Toad added.

"Can't you see the lights? Can't you hear the sounds?" Moose the Mouse asked.

"Yes, I see the lights, and I hear the sounds," Stanley the Turtle said.

"Then why such a frown; the carnival is in town?" Moose the Mouse asked.

"I am sad because I can't walk fast to get to the carnival in town. I walk slow, and I don't know if I will make it in time to enjoy the sights and sounds!" Stanley the Turtle confessed.

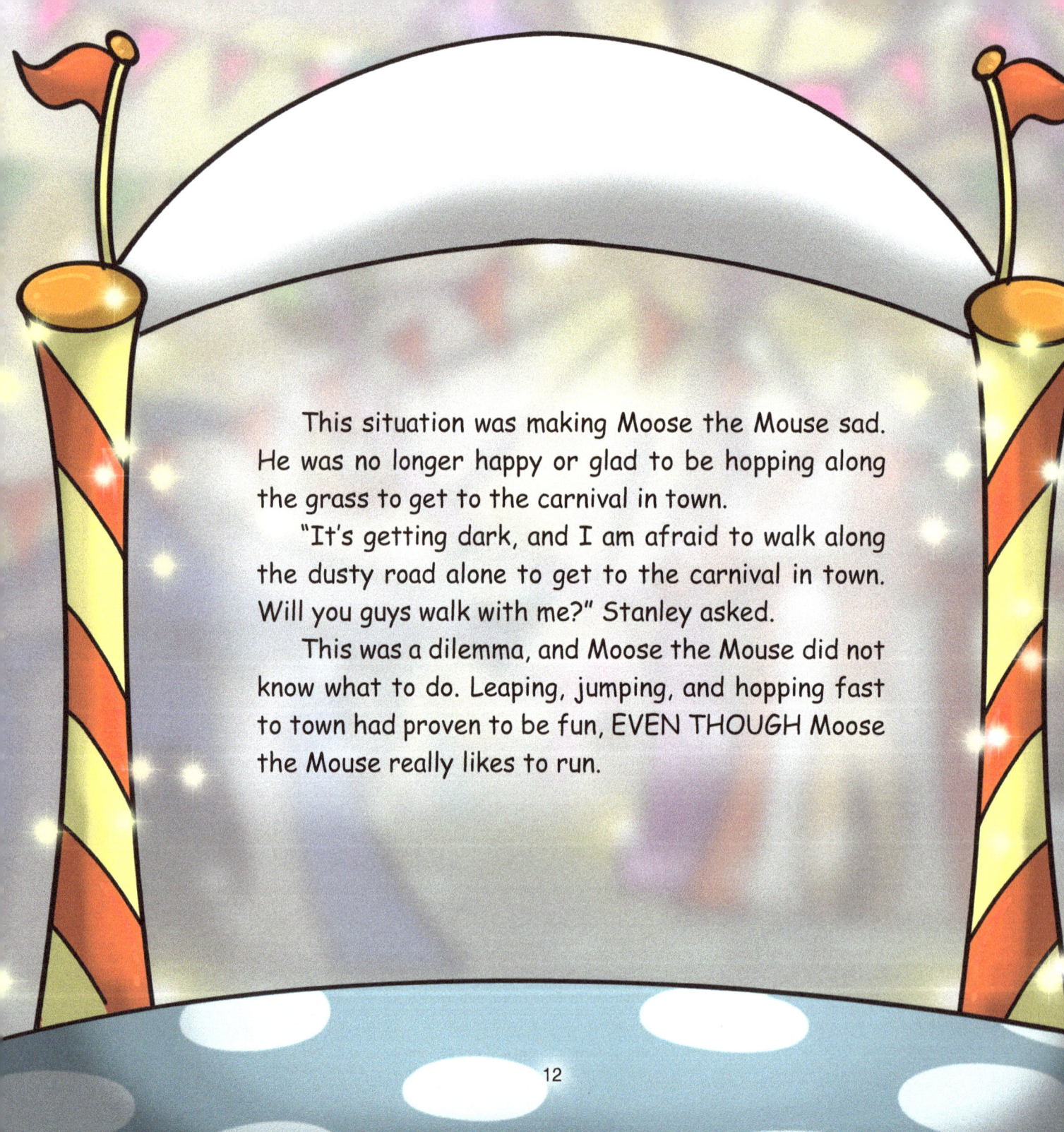

This situation was making Moose the Mouse sad. He was no longer happy or glad to be hopping along the grass to get to the carnival in town.

"It's getting dark, and I am afraid to walk along the dusty road alone to get to the carnival in town. Will you guys walk with me?" Stanley asked.

This was a dilemma, and Moose the Mouse did not know what to do. Leaping, jumping, and hopping fast to town had proven to be fun, EVEN THOUGH Moose the Mouse really likes to run.

Stanley the Turtle could not run, or leap or jump nor hop fast. Walking slow was going to be a challenging task for the four friends who just wanted to get to the carnival and have fun!

13

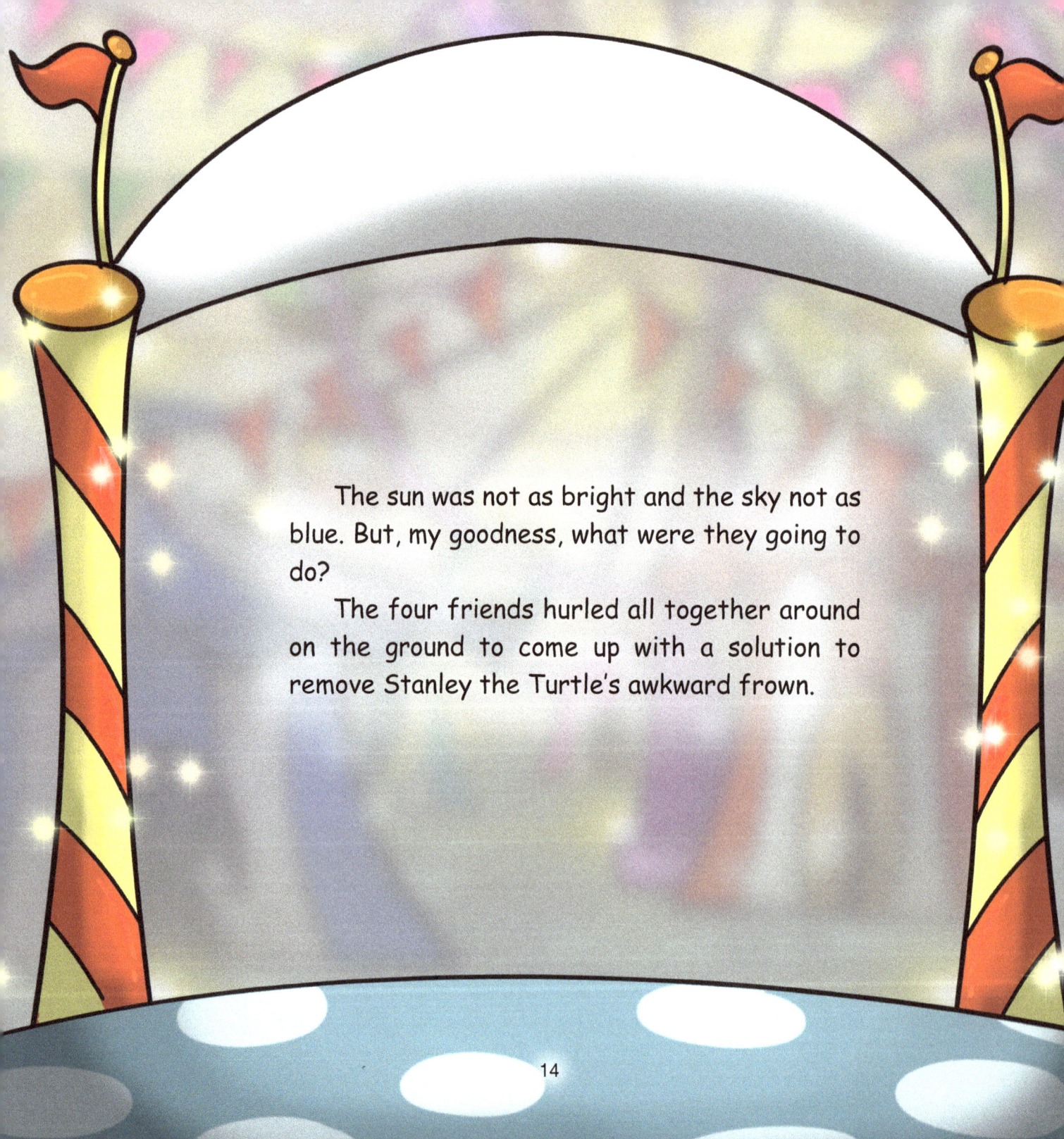

The sun was not as bright and the sky not as blue. But, my goodness, what were they going to do?

The four friends hurled all together around on the ground to come up with a solution to remove Stanley the Turtle's awkward frown.

After discussing the situation among themselves, it was decided the four friends would not leave Stanley the Turtle all alone to walk to the carnival in town.

"Katie the Kangaroo will carry you in her pouch to get you to the carnival in town," Moose the Mouse told Stanley the Turtle.

This immediately removed Stanley the Turtle's frown!

17

Moose the Mouse likes to run because running is fun.

The five friends with Stanley the Turtle, securely tucked inside Katie the Kangaroo's pouch, began running fast along the dusty road to get to the carnival in town.

They made it to the carnival in town, and Kitty the Kitten was still waiting for Moose the Mouse there.

The six friends were all together and having so much fun even as the sun began to go down; they were so happy to be at last at the carnival in town.

19

THE END

Imagine with Imagination!

A child's imagination is a gift from God. Let them pretend, have fun, think, and grow while learning about life along the way.

G.E. MILLER

About the Author

Born on October 25, 1956, in Gary, Indiana, G. E. Miller (Gwendolyn Elizabeth) had a vivid imagination from the start. By the 6th grade, she discovered she had a reading disability and read only by memorizing words that she'd heard.

Her parents aggressively began working with her to help improve her reading skills. After school, she came home to a room dedicated to her where she'd read out loud by herself. Her father gave her a dictionary, paper, and a pencil and instructed her to write down every word she could not pronounce while reading. After reading, she had to look up those words, write down the definition, and practice pronunciation.

By the time Gwen reached Junior High School, she was reading everything in sight. A need for writing emerged, and Gwen soon began writing poems. Her weekly allowance was used to buy paper, pens, and pencils. Joining the Gary Workshop Writers Group (Gary, Indiana), Gwen read many of her poems at the monthly readings. After graduating college, earning a B.A. in Communications in 1980, Gwen relocated to Little Rock, Arkansas.

Married to Larry S. Miller, the two have two children: LaShae and Glen and three grandchildren: Jason, Jeremiah, and Jada. In addition to her own biological children, Gwen has six stepchildren and fifteen step grandchildren.

A fellow writer once told her, "When it's time for you to fly, you will fly!"

Lightning Source UK Ltd.
Milton Keynes UK
UKHW051945041021
391649UK00002B/86